nF421439

(Guru) Arjan Dev Ji's elder brother Prithi Chand was married to Bibi Karmo in village Hehar, district Lahore. Baba Mahadev had refused to marry. When (Guru) Arjun Dev Ji was eleven years old, Guru Amar Das made up his mind to marry his youngest twin alive.

Krishna Chand, one of his beloved devotees, lived in the village of Mau (Doaba). He often came to serve the Guru. Once he came with his family, he was accompanied by his youngest daughter Ganga Devi. The Guru was very pleased to see the love, politeness and good manners of that girl. The Guru called Bhai Krishan Chand on the same day and asked for his daughter's relationship with his twin Guru Arjan. What more could Bhai Krishan Chand need? He spoke very happily, Maharaj! This is our luck, if my daughter gets a chance to serve the Guru's house then what could be bigger than this. I approve of this relationship. I have seen (Guru) Arjun Dev, he is a divine light.

After a few days the relationship was settled and the date of marriage was fixed . Preparations for the wedding began at the Guru's house. Guru Amar Das and (Guru) Ramdab engaged in wedding preparations. Because the river was coming along the way, the whole group was ready to go on horseback. Guru Amar Das called his grandson to him and adorned himself with a turban and sehra. E: Crossing the river Beas, Janj reached the village of Mau. All the men and women of the village came out of the village to greet him. One of our requests is that it is customary in this village that the bridegroom must first chase the horse and pierce it with a sharp spear. We did not want to impose this condition on ourselves, but this ritual has been going on since ancient times. On hearing this, the Guru burst out laughing and said, "Those great men! You have kept us as Sadh. We will enter the village only after digging this nail. Where is that nail?

The chief saw a nail made from a juniper tree driven into the field. They were all armed and had spears and kirpans. (Guru) Arjun Dev was given a spear. He grabbed his spear and chased his horse very fast and for the first time he nailed it and surprised all the people of the village. They thought that Eddie, an 11-year-old boy, would not be able to pull the trigger quickly. Even the warriors here were very happy and applauded this (Guru) Arjun Dev's aim. Guru Amar Das and (Guru) Ram Das blessed their brave child. Janjha then dismounted and the villagers took one horse at a time for fodder. When Janjh gathered, Bhai Krishan Chand came with a necklace to meet his cousin. (Guru) Ramdas and Bhai Krishan Chand met embracing. Then they took them all to their homes. After going home and eating and drinking, Bibi Ganga Devi and Guru Arjan Dev got married according to the Gur Maryada. The next day Barat reached Goindwal with Dolly. The two became a unique couple. The whole city rejoiced.

(Guru) Arjan Dev Ji was born on 15th April 1563 AD at Goindval Sahib. His mother's name was Bibi Bhani and his father's name was Guru Ram Das. Because Bibi Bhani was the daughter of Guru Amar Das, she looked like his grandfather. At that time Guru Ram Das had not yet become a Guru and was only serving the Guru. When Guru Amar Das found out that a third son had been born in his daughter's house, he went to see his granddaughter! At first glance, he said, "He will be a heavy man. Guru Amar Das loved his twin very much. So (Guru) Arjun Dev was also eager to visit him. They usually came to the Guru's house to play. Once, while he was playing, his mattress slipped under Guru Amar Das's bed. The Guru was resting at that time. When Guru Arjan Dev got out of bed to pick up the ball, the bed was lifted and Guru Ji fell asleep. Seeing the bed moving, he said instinctively;

"What kind of a big man is this?

While the Guru was saying these words, his daughter Bibi Bhani also reached there. She began to say, "This is your granddaughter if granddaughter." When Guru Ji heard these words, he again said, "Come to us from today and we will teach you Punjabi and Gurbani, we will teach Raag Vidya."

He also instructed Bibi Bhani to come to him daily with the child. The Guru was then four years old. He read with great interest and soon became an expert in raga vidya. When Guru Ji realized that Guru Ji has become proficient in learning and can sing every raga in a very beautiful voice then he hired Baba Mohri Ji to teach him mathematics. Baba Mohri was an expert in mathematics, so he made (Guru) Arjun Dev a good expert in mathematics. Pandit Beni was given the responsibility of teaching Hindi and Sanskrit. Due to the Muslim rule at that time, Persian was the official language.

So a Persian cleric was appointed to teach them Persian. Guru Arjan completed all kinds of studies by the age of ten.

But most of all he loved Gurbani very much, he would memorize Gurbani orally and recite it to his father Sri Ram Das Ji in the evening. (Guru ram dass ji. Would have been delighted to see such expertise in his rag vidya (Guru) Arjun Dev was also very fond of horse riding and spear throwing. When he went for a walk with his father and brothers in the morning, he would learn every trick of horse riding. Sometimes there was a spear fight between the brothers. Although Baba Mahadev was not interested in it but when his elder brother Prithi Chand lost to him he would be very sad. Because he saw that at the age of ten he had become a good scholar, a good horseman, and a skilled archer.

(Guru) Arjun Dev Ji also had great respect for Baba Mohan, he considered him a Puran Sant. He also loved his parents very much. He always stayed with them and obeyed their every command. Mata Bhani taught him to follow his will and Guru Ram Das established true service.

Reunion with Mian Mir was done bu guru ji

When Guru Ram Dass ji realized that the time was coming for his lord to merge with the race, he too, like the first Guru sahibs, decided to test his successor. In those days there was a marriage of sons of Bhai Sihari Mal, a relative of Guru Ram Das in Lahore. An invitation came to Guru Sahib to attend this wedding But Guru Sahib did not want to attend that wedding. He thought that his Sikh service in Lahore had increased so much. That marriage will be difficult to handle. He thought that he would take care of a son to attend the wedding. This will make it clear which of their sons is obedient. The son who agrees to go will be assured that he will not come to Amritsar without their permission. This will further reveal who is sincerely obedient. In this way he put up a comfortable paper for the exam.

First he called Baba Prithi Chand and ordered to attend the wedding. But he broke down and replied that he could not leave such a big business. Then he called his second son Maha Dev but he did not agree. He would say that he is a celibate and has forgotten the relationships of the world. He does not consider anyone as his relative. Then he (Guru) called Arjun Dev and gave this order. He immediately agreed. When he started to leave, Guru Ji said that when we do not call, he will not come back.

(Guru) Arjun Dev moved to Lahore, attended the wedding. After the marriage ended, they moved to Chuna Mandi, their father's ancestral home. When Guru Ram Dass ji visited Lahore, he turned it into a dharamsalal. Here Guru Arjan himself used to perform kirtan and katha every day. His voice was very melodious and he played all the instruments. The beloved of the Guru's house rejoiced. Day by day the number of sangat began to increase.

Lahore was a city of pious fakirs. During the day he would take some of his companions with him to visit the eminent saints and fakirs. In those days, Sai Mian Mir was considered a very revered saint

Used to go From great rulers to kings came to worship him. Guru Ji reached his dera to meet Sai Mian Mir. Lord Nanak's Guru Nanak too

Had a lot of love for his followers. When he found out (Guru Arjan Dev is the son of Guru Ram Das, the founder of Amritsar city), he lovingly seated him by his side. (Guru) Arjan Dev Ji used to visit him frequently now, after which he also met Shah Bilawal, Shah Hussain, Chhajju Bhagat, Kahna Bhagat and Peelu Bhagat. A long time passed, but he was not called back by the Guru. Finally he wrote a letter and sent it to Amritsar through one of his Sikhs. But Prathi Chand did not allow him to go to the Guru. He wrote the second letter and was taken care of by Prithi Chand. After this he wrote the third letter and asked his Sikh to hand over the letter to Guru Ji. He then asked the Sikh where the other two letters had gone. The Sikh said that the first letters were given to Prithi Chand. Gone. The Guru finally sent a Sikh to search his house and received the letters. (Guru) Arjun Dev succeeded in Khiya and Guru Ji installed him on the Guruship.

Guru Ram Dass ji handed over the throne to Guru Arjan, assuring the sangat that Guru Arjan was his form. All they have to do is accept the Guru and not follow anyone else. The next day Guru Ram Das went to Goindval. He was accompanied by Guru Arjan and other Sikhs. Stayed there one night and the next day merged in the light of the Lord After completing the last rites, Guru Arjan came to Amritsar.

Here again the teachings of Guru Ram Dass ji was followed. Every morning there would be kirtan of Bani and Guru Arjan would recite and preach to the sangat. | At that time Satta and his son Balvand used to perform kirtan in Darbar. The Guru and the sangat would be very pleased to hear his beautiful kirtan. One day Satta said to Guru Ji, "Maharaj, my daughter is getting married, help us a little. Guru Ji said," Don't worry, whatever is offered today will be given to you. After the end of the evening kirtan, all the offerings that came, were put in his lap. But when they counted Maya, the amount became very small. The offering was very low that day. He was very sad to see a small amount.

When Prithi Chand found out, he wanted to take advantage of such an opportunity. He met Balwand at the same time and said to them, This offering comes only because of your kirtan. If you stop doing kirtan then the Guru will not have the pleasure of a jhang.

Satta and Balwand came to the rescue of Prithi Chand. They passed the Guru and began to speak loudly against the Guru's house. They even said that Sangars come here because of our kirtan, if we don't come then no one should call you Guru. The Guru explained to them very politely, but they began to speak louder. When they did not keep quiet, the Guru said to the sangat, "They have slandered Guru Nanak's house, so do not bow down to them. The Guru himself knew how to play instruments and perform kirtan. So he picked up the instrument and started doing kirtan. When the sangat heard his kirtan, Anandmai reached in amazement He had never heard such a beautiful kirtan. When

When Satta and Balvand found out that Guru Sahib himself had started doing kirtan and sangats started coming more than before, he was very sorry.
Amir told him to go to Lahore with Bhai Ladhe Parupkari, he can help you. Listening to his talk, Bhai Landhe said, "You have done a very bad thing, you have slandered the Guru's house. I can accept your point but Guru Ji has also laid down a very big condition that whoever comes with their recommendation will be blackened and his donkey will be blown up. But they keep saying that they can't change what you say. At last Bhai Landhe turned his face and mounted a donkey and fell in front of them. Arriving at Amritsar, he mounted a donkey and came to Guru ka Mahal. The Guru recognized Bhai Landhe. The Guru began to say, "Bhai Lodhia, you have come to order them, but you know that they have slandered the Guru's house." If they now want to forgive themselves, then praise Nanak with the same language with which they have slandered the house, then let their illness be cured! "They both agreed and Guru Ghan Guru Granth Sahib Pages 988 to 988 are recorded in Ramkali Raga of Uttar Pradesh.

Bhai Manjh was a wealthy landowner from Kangmai village in Hoshiarpur district. Once Bhai Manjh went on a journey to Nihe Pir with a group of his companions. While he was returning, he met a Sikh and had the opportunity to listen to Guru Nanak's hymns. He was very impressed by Gurbani and expressed his desire to see the Guru seated on the throne of Guru Nanak. He was told that Guru Arjan was imparting spiritual knowledge in the form of the fifth Nanak at Amritsar.

Coming to Amritsar, he saw that the Guru's Sikhs were engaged in service with great humility, devotion and love. Construction work was also underway. He was very happy to see the sarovar and when he heard the glory of that sarovar of Amrit, he took bath with great devotion. Then he worshiped Guru Darbar and listened to divine kirtan He was overjoyed to hear the kirtan and made up his mind to become a Sikh. He was delighted to see the Guru and pleaded, "Maharaj! I want to be your own Sikh, have mercy on me. ' The Guru said, 'I am a servant of Sakhi Sarwar but it is not easy to be a Sikh. Sikhi is thinner than hair and sharper than the edge of a dagger. The path of Sakhi Sarwari is easy. To become a Sikh one has to give up anger, greed, attachments, ego and arrogance.

Bhai Manjh again politely requested, "Maharaj, I am ready to give up everything. But the Guru said, "You can do everything but Sikhi cannot survive without learning!" The last words pierced Bhai Manjh and took him away. He understood the real thing. He returned to his village. He demolished the Pirkhana built in his house. The whole village turned against him Chaudharpuna was taken away from him. | Finally he came to Amritsar. Visited Guru Arjan Dev Ji, bowed but did not say anything Like the rest of the Sikhs, they too joined the service. He would go into the forest and cut wood. People would spend all day in some kind of service. Once he was coming to Amritsar carrying a load of wood

There was a strong wind, and there was darkness all around. In that darkness he fell into a well. But he did not allow the wood to get wet. He kept it on his head and started reading. When he did not reach the camp at night, the other Sikhs became anxious and set out to find him. From a well came the sound of Gurbani page. When he saw Bhai Manjh standing in the well resting on a pand of wood, he was reciting. They immediately ran to the Guru's camp and brought the ropes. Hanging the rope, he told Bhai Manjh to come out with the rope. But Bhai Manjh said, "First take out this dry wood, then I will come out too." When Guru Ji found out about this incident, he too reached the well. Seeing Guru Ji at the well, Bhai Manjh fell at Guru's feet. Guru Ji said, "Bhai Manjh, your earnings are now successful, ask for something." Bhai Manjh said, "Guru Ji! Forgive me that I may never forget the Naam Simran and fill my pockets with Sidak Daan. Guru Ji was very pleased to hear this from Bhai Manjh and said. . Manjh Pyara Guru Ke, Gur Manjh Pyara
Manjh Guru ka Bohitha, Jag Langhan Hara - Keeping in view the efforts of Bhai Manjh, Guru Ji sent him to his village as Pracharak.

Bhai Budhu Shah was a government contractor in Lahore. His real name was Sadhu. He used to sell bricks to the government by laying bricks from the workers and then baking them in the fields.

He was also a great lover of Guru Ghar. While Guru Arjan was staying at Lahore, he became very devoted to him.

Once the bricks were laid and when they were placed in the vats, they requested the Guru Sahib to pray for the bricks to come out well. He set up a langar in his mansion and invited the Guru and other sangat. While the sangat was eating langar, Laghu Patolia, who later became famous as Bhai Kamalia, went there to eat langar. But seeing his torn clothes, the servants would not let him in. He kept shouting but no one listened to him. After eating in the langar, when a Sikh was asked to pray and when the Sikh said in the prayer that the bricks in the avas should be fully cooked, Bhai Kamalia shouted from outside, "They will remain raw, they will remain raw." I am starving. His servants did not let me in and said that the langar was over. This poor man will surely die and the bricks will remain raw. After the end of the prayer, when Bhai Budhu Shah told Guru Ji about these bad words of Bhai Kamalia, Guru Ji said, "The bricks will remain raw now. Because what a poor person says is not in vain. Your servants saw his torn clothes and did not let him in, but he is a sincere devotee and carefree. Bhai Budhu Shah was overwhelmed with anxiety and told Abhay Guru that ours. There is no benefit in praying? The Guru said, "A sincere prayer is never in vain, but the word of the poor is to be fulfilled. The benefit of our prayers will be that even the raw yellow bricks of your kilns will be sold at the price of hard bricks.

The Guru's words also came true. It rained so hard at that time that all the people's houses collapsed. Even a wall of the government fort collapsed. The governor tried hard to find solid bricks but could not find them

But it was also important to build the wall with protection in mind. So they bought Bhai Budhu Shah's raw pinni bricks at the same price as the fixed bricks.

Bhai Bhudu Shah was very pleased with the Gur's words and as a token of gratitude he came to the Guru with many presents. Seeing the gifts, the Guru said, 'You should give these gifts to Bhai Kamaliya, whom you kept hungry that day, or don't bring langar. Are forms. You take Bhai Landhe and meet Bhai Kamalia and apologize by placing food presents in front of him! If he forgives you, then your bricks will definitely come out from now on! " He was very happy to see the gifts and forgave Bhai Budhu Shah on the condition that the servants who did not let him in must be punished.

Before Guru Amar Das passed away, Guru Ram Das was told to establish the city of Amritsar, Amrit Sarovar and Harimandar Sahib but due to lack of time, Guru Ram Das could only get the city of Amritsar and Amrit Sarovar constructed. He had erected a platform in the middle of the Amrit Sarovar where kirtan was performed at the Darbar. When Guru ram Dass ji was about to merge with the Lord, he urged Guru Arjan to build a Harimandar in the middle of the Amrit Sarovar where kirtan was performed at all times. Guru Arjan, in obedience to that order, decided to build a temple on the same Bada as no other temple had. Where there is nothing but Kirtan, only Simran is Simran. First Guru Ji made his own plan for construction. He thought that the four doors of the Golden Temple should be kept, these doors should not be in any particular direction but one door between the two directions. When Guru Sahib stayed in Lahore for two years, he fell in love with Sai Mian Mir. Sai Ji also became Anin Bhagat of Guru Ghar. When the question of laying the foundation of Harimandar Sahib arose, Guru Ji chose Sai Mian Mir as the most suitable and suitable great man to lay the foundation. Sai Mian Mir was an ally of Hindus and Muslims. They bowed down to him, from the lowest to the lowest. The Guru himself reached Lahore and explained in detail to Sai Mian Mir the construction of the Golden Temple. He requested them to lay the foundation stone. Sai Mian Mir immediately agreed and came to Amritsar with the Guru. He laid the foundation stone of Sri Harmandir Sahib on 3 October 1588. Sai Mian Mir laid four bricks in four directions, one between the four, on the wrist of the foundation. Guru Sahib then called all the masons and explained to them the plan of the Golden Temple. | The chair of the Golden Temple was raised above the water of the sarovar and arches were built below it. To the east Har Ki Pauri was built and Parkarmas were prepared on all sides. Guru Sahib himself used to get the construction done under his supervision. Any inferior Item not found.

The Guru would sit under the cardamom berry and watch.

The construction of the Golden Temple took a full three years. Upon completion, the Guru uttered the following words in the Suhi Raag as a thank you:

ਸੰਤਾ ਕੇ ਕਾਰਜਿ ਆਪਿ ਖਲੋਇਆ ਹਰਿ ਕੰਮੁ ਕਰਾਵਣੀ ਆਇਆ ਰਾਮ॥ ॥ ਧਰਤਿ ਸੁਹਾਵੀ ਤਾਲੁ ਸੁਹਾਵਾ ਵਿਚਿ ਅੰਮ੍ਰਿਤ ਜਲੁ ਛਾਇਆ ਰਾਮ

After the construction of the Golden Temple, the daily Darbar started appearing here. The kirtans make the sangat happy by performing kirtan. The creation of the Golden Temple was also supernatural. When Muslims bow their heads to the west

That the Hindus used to pray to the east. But the doors of the Golden Temple were neither east nor west. All four doors remain open at all times and every character is free to come. No one is restricted. This is the first place of worship that is lower than the earth. You have to go down the stairs to visit. Meaning first one has to say arrogance and then one has to go with humility.

The Guru decided to visit all of Majha to curb the preaching of Sakhi Sarvars. He reached Khara village via Jandiala, Khadur, Goindwal, Chola Sahib and Khanpur villages. He camped outside the salty village after seeing a beautiful place. There was a pool of pure water and there were orchards of mangoes, berries, peaches, etc. all around. The Guru made up his mind to establish a town on such a beautiful place. Through his Sikhs he bought the required land. To make that water tank a permanent sarovar as well as a dharamshala, he had bricks made.

One day while the service of fixing the sarovar was being done, a jogi came there. The jogi told Guru Sahib that he had a bundle of ashes. The glory of this ash is that if it is rubbed with iron it becomes silver and if it is rubbed with copper it becomes gold. On hearing this, Guru Sahib asked if there was any other praise in it. Guru Sahib grabbed the bundle from him and threw all the ashes into the sarovar. The Jogi was very sad to see this, but Guru Ji said that Maya creates ego, anger and greed in a human being, but it is a work of public welfare. Whoever bathes in this sarovar, his disease will be cured.

One day the Guru ji was going for a walk when on the way he saw four men carrying a weeping man lying on a bed. Guru Ji stopped them and asked, where are you taking this sick person and who is this? | He said, "This is our father and he is the Chaudhary of Muradpur village. Leprosy to them

The disease has caused a lot of pain. Now they say let them cry in the river Beas. That is why we are going to water them in the river Beas. The Guru ordered them not to throw Chaudhary into the river Beas. Bring them with me and bathe in the sarovar. By taking a bath for two or three days and listening to the recitation of Gurbani, it will get better

Hearing these words of Guru Sahib, Chaudhary's sons were very happy and brought Chaudhary's bed and placed it on the bank of the sarovar. Then, according to the order, he gave the sarovar to his father

. After taking a bath on the first day, Chaudhary felt himself relaxed. His wounds, which were leaking and painful, healed. He used to listen to kirtan every morning and evening and take bath in the sarovar. Within a few days, he was completely healed. (After Chaudhary's leprosy was cured, Guru Ji opened a leper's house there, where he came from different parts of the country and started living in a leper's house. Used to go Some settled in Tarn Taran. The construction of the sarovar was not completed when Amanat Khan forcibly took away the bricks from the Guru's presence. He was building a lighthouse in memory of his father. When the Maharaja came to know about this, he said, "These bricks will be used for the purpose for which they were made." Just as the bricks are gone with the force of force, so the bricks will come back with the force of force. Were brought in the processions back by sardar budh singh and jassa singh ramgarhia.

After the construction of Tarn Taran, Guru Ji made Doaba the center of his preaching. Coming to Doaba, Guru Ji realized that a city should be established here too so that the preaching of Sikhism could be facilitated! While they were staying at Dalle, Nawab Nazim Khan of Jalandhar came to visit them. He was very pleased to see the Guru's teachings and the common langar. He implored Guru Sahib, 'Maharaj! Which religion is better then Guru Ji replied, "Ajab is all good, it is a matter of deeds. | Later, Nawab Nazim Khan requested that a city be established near Jalandhar where he could stay for the welfare of humanity. He also said that he has a lot of land near Jalandhar and he can give it to them for settlement But the Guru said that they could not get the land for free, we would pay the price so that the town could have an independent existence. The Nawab agreed and the Guru returned to Kartarpur.

Guru Ji laid the foundation stone of the town in his own hands in December 1984 by leasing the land in his name. After constructing some residential houses, Guru Ji brought a big well He named this well Gangsar. When the construction of the well was completed, Guru Ji allowed all the sangat that no one needs to go to Ganga now. Ganga flows in this well. The bath of Gangsar is better than the bath of Ganga. A Sikh expressed some doubts about this and was shown the Ganga flowing in the well.

The construction of Kartarpur was in full swing. The Guru entrusted the construction to Bhai Kalyan and Bhagat. After staying there for some time, he came to Amritsar.

One day Mata Ganga ji's maid was scattering on the stitches to dry the sewn clothes. The Sikh Sanghars donated very valuable clothes to the Guru's house. When Pithi Chand's wife saw these clothes, she got burnt. She started saying to Prithi Chand, "Look how many precious clothes have been donated by the sangat to Arjun Dev's house, no one asks us. On hearing this, Pithi Chand said, "Good people, don't worry,

Guru Arjan Dev has no son, he has to go childless. All these precious things are to be given to your son. So take a few more days with more patience. The fact is that Guru Sahib had been married for twelve years but had no children at home.

The servant of Mata Ganga was secretly listening to this whole conversation. She told the whole story to Mata Ji. Mata Ji was very sad to hear this. Mata Ganga Ji told all this to Guru Arjan Dev Ji and said, What is the use of this life for me?

The Guru said, "There is nothing lacking in the Guru's house. Go to Brahmgiani Baba Buddha, please him and ask for the gift of a son."

The very next day, Mata Ganga prepared a very good dish and reached Bir with some of the inhabitants in a chariot.

Baba Buddha ji was born at Bhai Sugha ji in the womb of Mata Gauran ji in village Kabunangal, district Amritsar on 7 Katak Sammat 1563. The parents named themselves Buda. When he was seven or eight years old, he used to take part in the work of his parents. He used to take the cattle out to graze outside. One day Guru Nanak and Bhai Mardanan came to Kathunangal while preaching and they set up a Diwan outside the village. The old man left the cattle and went to the Guru's Diwan He was very impressed by the Guru's discourse and remained seated even after the conclusion of the Diwan. Guru Nanak called him to his side and said, "What is your name?" He gave his name as Buda. Seeing her love, Guru Ji asked her from her parents.

.

Guru Ji used to call him Buddha because of his very wise words at a young age and his name became Baba Buddha. Going to Kartarpur, he rendered great service to the Guru's house and also to the extent of Prabhu Simran. He studied hard and memorized the entire Bani of Guru Nanak Sahib. When Guru Nanak had to choose his successor, only two Sikhs could pass the test. One was Guru Angad Dev Ji and the other was Baba Buddha Ji. When Guru Nanak Dev Ji asked Baba Buddha to fulfill the responsibility of the Guruship, Baba Buddha humbly requested, "Give me the gift of Maharaj Gursikhi and give me the gift that you will never leave me. Guru Nanak was very pleased with him and said, "We will never leave you and if you do not want to become a Guru then from now on you will be considered as the real Guru who will accept you." You and your heirs will be the guardians of the Guru's house. "Thus Guru Nanak blessed him with infinite blessings. History testifies that no one in the world can match the service rendered by him to the Guru's house later. By tilak Guru Angad, he sealed the Guruship. When the circle of Mai Bharai at Guru Angad Dev Sanghar disappeared, he revealed it and took it to Khadur Sahib to make it a new center of Sikhism and started the work of propagating Sikhism.

Guru Amar Dass, Guru Ram Dass, Guru Arjan Dev and Guru Hargobind became the guarantors of the Guru's title. In those days Baba Buddha used to stay at Guru Ki Bir! There he supervised the care of the buffaloes and cows of the Guru's house The milk of these buffaloes and cows came for the Guru's langar. When Mata Ganga with her companions ascended to God and approached the Guru's Bir, Baba Ji saw the dust of the chariots flying and said, "Who is this coming?" Baba Buddha sehaj subhaa said, "Guru ka mahilaan ki bhajr pagi hai? Maara Ganga ji baba buddha ji ka achh bachan sabhe yaar rabh hal hai." He returned to Amritsar and told the whole story to Guru Arjan Dev Ji. Put all these things on your head and go. This is what Mata Ganga Ji did. When Baba Buddha Ji saw Mata Ji coming, he said, They seem to have brought it. Then they began to eat the missi roti and while giving the ganda they gave the gift that in their house a sacrificial son will be born who will behead the Mughals as if I am touching this mattress. "

When Prithi Chand and his wife Karmo found out that Mata Ganga was about to become a mother, they were very sad. Jealous, they kept saying bad words all the time. There was always trouble in the house. The Guru thought of staying away from his jealous and jealous brother. They moved to Wadali Nagar, four miles from Amritsar. The whole town loved the Guru's house very much and they were very happy to have the Guru's Wadali settled down. When the sangat found out, Darbar started appearing there and kirtan started flowing!

According to the gift of Baba Buddha, Guru Hargobind was born on 6 Har Sammat 1652 AD in the village of Wadali. The family and the sangat were overjoyed to receive this information. On the other hand, Baba Prithi Chand and his wife Karamo's heart ached. | When Baba Buddha found out, he walked from Guru's Bir to Wadali village. Baba Ji congratulated Guru Arjan Dev on the birth of Sahibzada and prayed to God to grant him long life. After seeing Sahibzada, he named him Hargobind.

Here Guru Ji was doing alms to the people, on the other hand Baba Pithi Chand was thinking of tricks to kill Sahibzada Hargobind.

He first bought the midwife by paying a large sum of money and asked her to poison her body and suck the Sahibzada. The family relied on him. She took the child to the roof of the toy and began to poison the child's mouth. But Bal Hargobind started crying loudly. When Mata Ganga ji and the other accused found out about Khidavi's deed, she admitted that she was sent by Prithi Chand out of greed. Due to the poisoning of the forest, he died there. Gone. But where Prithi Chand was about to retreat, he sent a snake charmer to drop a venomous snake at Hargobind showing off the snake show. Reached Guru Ji's house playing Spera Bean 4 All the Sevaks and Mata Ji along with the boy Hargobind came to see the show. The boy smiled when he saw the snake

Then he sent a snake to him! When Sahibzada saw the snake, he was not scared but grabbed it by the head and killed it by rubbing its head with the ground. All of them were amazed to see this amazing miracle.

Then Prithi Chand bought Sahibzada's toy Brahmin. He was told to put poison in the yoghurt and give it to the child to drink. But when he got poison and started giving yoghurt to Sahibzada, he refused to drink and started screaming. Everyone in the house came there. He placed the yoghurt in front of a dog and the dog died in agony. At the same time the Brahmin got such a pain that he too died in agony.

When all the times of Prithi Chand were vacated, he planned to kill one of Sahibzada's peers Nand Ram. He took Nand Ram's uncle in his arms and asked him to make a two pocket shirt for Nand Ram. Then he said that Nand Ram should have a good sweet in one pocket and a poisoned sweet in the other. Thus when they go to play Nand Ram eats good sweets himself and feeds the poisoned Sahibzada. When the two peers went to play, Nand Ram forgot which mini was good and which was bad. He ate that poisonous dessert and gave it to the good Sahibzada. Nand Ram died on the spot.

When Guru Ji realized that while living in Wadali some or the other incidents keep happening, he came to Amritsar with his family. Due to the attacks on Sahibzada, the Sikh Sangat cursed Baba Prithi Chand so much that he left his camp and returned to his father-in-law's village.

Like Amritsar, they built Harimandar Sahib there and started sitting with dirt But where would the sangats be caught?

When Pichand saw that the means of earning were running out, he made plans to expel Guru Arjan from Amritsar with the help of that government. He went to Lahore and started meeting the rulers. He would come to them with many valuable gifts and presents. Many rulers became his personal friends. Baba Mahadev, of course, was obsessed with the sorrows and joys of the world. He says the Turks themselves will be destroyed.

Prithi Chand once got the news that a friend of his, Hakim Sulhi Khan, was coming to his father-in-law's village Hehar. Prithi Chand humbly approached him and repeated his grief. Sulhi Khan listened to her complaint patiently and said, "Look! I am still busy with very important things. So I would instruct my nephew Sulbi Khan to go to Amritsar and bring back to you the lost right to the throne. Taking Sulhi Khan's message, he personally met Sulbi Khan. But Sulbi Khan used to fight when he reached Beas and before crossing the river he got into a quarrel with one of his officials Hasan Ali. Hassan Ali was a strong warrior Angered, he removed Sulbi Khan's neck. When Prithi Chand found out that Sulbi Khan had been killed, he was deeply saddened. All his plans were thwarted. He passed Sulhi Khan and begged and persuaded him to attack Amritsar. Prithi Chand promised to give him a lot of money. When the Sikhs came to know of this news, they requested the Guru to send the news to Emperor Akbar immediately. But the Guru did not accept this and said, "We must trust God and should abide in his will.

Sulhi Khan arrived at Hehar with his troops. Prithi Chand did him a great service. In the evening, Prithi Chand took him to see his newly started brick kiln. Sulhi Khan was very arrogant and conceited. He had a very good breed of horse. He also had great respect for that horse. When his horse approached the burning kiln, he was frightened by the flight of a bird and jumped, climbed over the wall of the kiln and fell into the burning kiln along with Sulhi Khan. Prithi Chand kept shouting and Sulhi Khan was burnt to ashes. This attempt of Prithi Chand also failed, the troops retreated to Lahore. They also reprimanded him for having to pay the price.

When Prithi Chand found out that the Mughal government had also turned against her, she sat down and did not try to do any mischief again.

Baba Prithi Chand, of course, had given up, but his son was preparing a granth which contained the Guru's Bani. He himself wrote the Bani under the name of Guru Nanak. In this way the Guru's Bani was mixed in such a way that it became difficult to judge between Sachchi Bani and Kachhi Bani. When Guru Arjan came to know about this, he decided to compile the Bani of all Gurus and devotees in one Granth in consultation with Bhai Gurdas and Baba Buddha. He entrusted Baba Buddha with the responsibility of Darbar Sahib and made up his mind to complete the work at Ramsar. He first built a sarovar at Ramsar and pitched tents on the banks of the sarovar.

Guru Nanak devoted all his Bani(holy teachings)to Guru Angad and Guru Angad incorporated his Bani in it and handed it over to Guru Amar Ds. Guru Amar D ji also composed his own Bani and before passing away he too had handed over his Bani and the Banis of the first Gur sahibs to Ram Dass ji and Gur Ram Dass ji also gave the Bani of all Gurus including his Bani to Guru Arjan dev Were gone Thus Guru Arjan had the handwritten hymns of all the Gurus. Guru Arjan arranged the entire Bani according to the ragas, but kept the Bani as it appeared. He sent Bhai Banno to Lahore to get a beautiful binding of the Bir. He also made a copy of the Bir at the time of binding of the Bir and Guru Sahib did not accept that Bir and cursed it to be salty Bir. When other devotees came to know that Guru Sahib was preparing a ganth in which the hymns of the devotees were also being included, many devotees came to Amritsar and met the Guru. But the Guru refused to record the words of such devotees which were not in accordance with the Guru's wishes. Thus Bhagat Kalan, Chhajju, Peelu and Shah Hussain returned disappointed.

It took three years to complete the Aad Granth. When the Bir was completed, messages were sent to distant Sikhs that the Bir of Adi Granth was being seated at Sri Harmandir Sahib on Bhadon Sudi Ekmat Sammat 1661. The sangats rushed to the spot. Addressing the sangat, Guru Ji said, "This Ganth has built a ship for swimming in the world ocean. Anyone who reads, listens, and ponders carefully will be saved!
The Bir was placed on the head of Baba Buddha and brought to Darbar Sahib. Baba Buddha was appointed the first granthi. This Granth at that time had 974 pages. Arriving at the Golden Temple, the Bir was placed on a decorated throne and Guru Ji asked Nau Baba Buddha Ji to take a speech. Baba Buddha took the sentence. Then when night fell, Baba Ji asked where the Granth Sahib should be rested at night. The Guru replied, "Spread new clothes on the newly made bed which is specially kept in my room." Thus at night the Adi Granth was rested on a new bed and the Guru himself made his bed on the ground.
This shows us how much Guru Ji respected Granth Sahib.

While Guru Ji was preparing the Bir of Granth Sahib, many devotees also brought their compositions to be included in this Granth. The Guru read those compositions with great affection but refused to include them as they did not suit the Guru's wishes. The other Bhagars then remained silent Kahn was Chandu's cousin in the relationship. So with the help of that Chandu, he gathered other fakirs and devotees to lodge a complaint with Emperor Akbar.
But he was still planning to die.
When the Brahmins found out about this, they spread the rumor that Bhagat Kane had been killed by Guru Arjan. He then prepared a complaint and wrote in it that Guru Arjan had prepared a Granth condemning the Muslim saints, prophets and Hindu incarnations and deities.
Emperor Akbar had met Guru Amar Das and Guru Ram Das, so he ignored the complaint. But he assured the Brahmins that whenever he came to Punjab, his complaint would be investigated. Some time later, when Akbar came to Batala, a delegation of Brahmins visited him again and reminded him of their complaint. Emperor Akbar sent a message to the Guru that he wanted to visit the dome he had created, so it should be sent to Batala. | By that time many copies of Ranth Sahib had been made. The Guru placed the Granth Sahib in a palanquin and sent it to Batala with Baba Buddha and Bhai Gurdas.
Akbar also summoned the Brahmins and other complainants and asked them to recite the Shabad from the Granth Sahib in a crowded court. When Baba Buddha Ji uttered this sentence, this Guruwak came out:
ਖਾਕ ੑਨੂਰ ਕਰਦੇ ਆਲਮ ਦੁਨੀਆਇ॥
ਚਸਮ ਦੀਦੰ ਫਨਾਇ॥ Akbar was very happy to hear these words but the complainants started saying that these were already marked, so it should be read from another page.

Akbar got into another game after hearing the three guruwaks uttered by baba budha ji. Dismissing the grievances, he said, "This Granth deserves less praise. Without Bandgi of Allah, I did not see anything else in it. No religion was slandered or insulted in it. In it an ah is praised. Akbar immediately got up from his seat and offered a hundred ashrafis and prostrated before the Granth Sahib. The complainants, embarrassed, slipped away from Akbar's wrath.

(Guru) Hargobind Sahib had a good stature at an early age. Everyone was impressed by his charming personality. When one of Akbar's Diwans, Chandu, asked some priests to find a bridegroom for his daughter, they wandered about and reached Amritsar. When they came to the Guru's court, they were astonished to see the aura of (Guru) Hargobind Sahib.
But when Chandu started sending Shagun, he said, "I accept the relationship, but you have put the brick in the attic hole. You did not do well.
Some Sikhs also went with the priests. When he heard these insulting words from Chandu, he became angry. He had already sent a Sikh to Amritsar. He met the Sikh Guru and said, "Chandu has called himself Mauri again and the Guru's house. So this relationship should not be accepted.

The Guru called Bhai Gurdas, Baba Buddha and other Sikhs and told them the whole story. All the Sikhs in unison said that this relationship should not be taken. | The next day when the Shagun was worshiped, Guru Ji flatly refused to take the Shagun When Chandu was told by the elders to return the shagun, Chandu became very angry and sent one lakh rupees to the Guru to give. But the Guru refused to accept the money and said that even if he wanted to give the wealth of the whole world, he would not accept it even then. | When Chandu realized that his daughter would remain a virgin all his life, he

He became very much against the Guru and kept inciting Jahangir against the Guru. | But Jahangir was against the Guru even before he became king. He had made up his mind to stop the preaching of Guru Nanak while Akbar was still alive In his autobiography (Tuzak), he writes, "By adapting many naive Hindus and bastard Muslims to his own ideas, he was beaten to death. The shop has been running for three or four generations. For a long time I wanted to close this fake shop or convert him to Islam. "

Thus Jahangir had made up his mind to martyr Guru Arjan even before the Chandu incident. He was just looking for an excuse. He was also found guilty of rebelling against his son Khusrau. Khusrau considered Guru Arjan as his mentor. As he was fleeing towards Kabul for fear of being caught, he stopped at Tarn Taran. He met Guru Arjan and tasted prasad in the langar.

Thus meeting the rebellious Khusrau to Guru Ji, Jahangir got a good excuse to martyr Guru Arjan Dev! Murtaza Khan, the ruler of Lahore, had already sent reports against the Guru. He also wrote to Jahangir that the Guru had blessed Khusrau and smeared his forehead. In his autobiography, Jahangir writes, "These days Khusrau crossed that path. This man Guru Arjan Dev Ji intended to meet Khusrau. Khusrau landed at that place and it happened where Guru Arjan was located. He came and saw her and met her. He said many things and put saffron on his forehead with his finger which Hindus call tilak and consider it as shagun. When this news reached my ears, I was well aware of his lies! I ordered that he (Guru Arjan Dev) be produced and his house, ghat, children be handed over to Murtaza Khan. His belongings were confiscated and he was ordered to be tortured to death.

Jahangir was deeply saddened by the fact that Muslims were becoming servants of Guru Arjan, so he forgot to kill the Guru. The Guru also knew the urgency of the times. Jahangir's views were also reaching him. He knew that the time of martyrdom was near. So he summoned Baba Buddha, Bhai Gurdas and other eminent Sikhs and on May 15, 1606, handed over the Guruship to Guru Hargobind. He preached to Guru Hargobind Sahib, "We preached Sikhism peacefully but now times have changed. Now there will be a war between good and evil. So you should tighten your belt now. Put on your armor and allow the Sikhs to take up arms

A few days later, Murtaza Khan arrested the Guru from Amritsar. The Guru was accompanied by five Sikhs on their own.

Arriving at Lahore, the Guru was presented at Jahangir's court. Jahangir asked many questions which Guru Ji answered appropriately He was also asked to include some words of praise for Muhammad in the Adi Granth Sahib, but the Guru flatly refused. He was then asked to convert to Islam. The Guru said that we can renounce the body but not the religion. When the Guru did not accept any condition, Jahangir ordered to be tortured and martyred.

Earlier, they were tortured by sitting in the hot sand of Har month. When Sai Mian Mir came to know about this incident, he met Jahangir. But Jahangir disobeyed. The Guru was then placed in a cauldron of boiling water. But they sat quietly with the Lord. Then hot sand was placed on the scorched body and placed on a hot plate. This filled their whole body with flu.

Be persecuted like this for five days. On the sixth day, i.e. May 30, 1606 AD, they were taken to the banks of river Ravi. There they were thrown into the river Ravi. The Guru was thus martyred by torture.

(Guru) Hargobind Sahib was born on 9 June 1595 AD in the village of Wadali, 4 miles from Amritsar. Guru Arjan was on a mission in Majha at that time. When he found out, he sent instructions to take full care of the child. He knew that his elder brother Prithi Chand Shrur would conspire and try to kill the boy. He was right. Prithi Chand hatched several conspiracies to kill the boy but could not do so. After staying in Wadali for some time, Guru Ji again took his family to Amritsar. Arrangements were made for Hargobind's education and training at Amritsar. Baba Buddha was called to Amritsar and under his supervision (Guru) Hargobind was taught literacy, wisdom and science. Along with this education, Bhai Jetha ji who was proficient in martial arts, taught spear throwing, archery, shooting, sword and gun wielding. Bhai Ganga Sehgal matured in horse riding. (Guru) Hargobind Sahib's body was very healthy and he used to do wrestling at an early age. He would also take down wrestlers older than his age. Baba Prithi Chand, as many attempts were made to kill the boy (Guru) Hargobind, the people of Amritsar turned against him and made his life miserable. Saddened, he left Amritsar for his father-in-law's village of Haihar. Going there he built his own separate Harimandar, but the people did not face him. | Along with armor, Guru Hargobind was deeply studying Gurbani. At an early age, he had memorized many verses. This was the reason why after becoming a Guru, when he was doing Katha, he was quoting many verses of Gurbani. At a very young age, his personality was very attractive. His passion was very strong and his daughter-in-law was sharp. In the words of Bhai Santokh Sigh, (Gur)) Hargobind's feet were like red lotus shells, the nails of his hands and feet were as delightful as a string of diamonds. Their legs were as beautiful as a betel nut tree and their ankles and knees were bulging and large. His chest was wide and his shoulders were high. Strictly on their side,

Strong and flexible like an elephant's trunk. Both his hands were like lotus and sprouted petals. His face was like the moon, his teeth were white and his lips were beautiful. His eyes were as sharp as the petals of a lotus which delighted the sangat with a single glance. Both things on his chin were soft, soft and round. On which the hanging coils were showered with splendor. Seeing their beauty, at the age of ten many relationships started coming. Chandu, who had the king's Diwan at Delhi, sent his priests to find a bride for his daughter. Hearing the splendor of Guru Arjan Dev Ji, he reached the court of Guru Sahib. Seeing the face of (Guru) Hargobind Sahib, he went to the fort. He (Chandu's daughter's relationship with Guru Hargobind was confirmed). But when Chandu started chanting Shagun, he said, "Prohat ji, you have not done well. After telling everything to Shagun, he turned it back. Later Chandu tried hard but Guru Ji did not agree. Thus Chandu became hostile to Guru's house. Jahangir's son Khusrau had revolted. On his way to Kabul, when he met Tarn Taran Guru Arjan, the report reached Jahangir. Jahangir was already against the Guru's house. So he called Guru Arjan to Lahore. Before leaving Amritsar for Lahore on 22 May 1606, Guru Arjan handed over the charge of the Guruship to Guru Hargobind. As he left, he said, "Arm yourself and make your Sikhs armed. These tyrants can no longer be confronted by becoming fakirs.

At that time Guru Ji was only eleven years old. Of course he was young in age but very big in intellect, courage, generosity, devotion and power. When Baba Buddha Ji put on a sword, it fell on the wrong side. When Baba Buddha Ji started taking it off, Guru Ji said bring another sword! They put the other sword on the other side! He said he would now wear only two swords. One sword belongs to Miri and one to Piri. Like the kings and emperors, they also wore turbans. The Guru's radiance shone like the sun at that time. After sitting on the throne, the Guru said, "From now on I will have a good weapon and a good horse. All Sikhs be armed. Exercise, play Gatka and go into the woods, play hunting I still need Sikh warriors the most. Whoever wants to be our Sikh, enlists in our army, here he will be taught to wield all kinds of weapons! "

Acknowledging the Guru's offer, the Sikhs began offering arms and horses to the Guru. Hundreds of Sikh warriors began to enlist in the Guru's army. The Guru made it clear to them that they would get Prasada from the langar both times and after six months they would get new clothes to wear. What more could the Sikhs want? They both listened to kirtan, practiced wielding weapons during the day, exercised and were getting healthier than before. They were not afraid of anyone. Their Guru was with them. He also went hunting with the Guru.

The Guru hired twenty-two leading men as his bodyguards. When some of the Pathans were driven out of the Mughal army, they came to the Guru.
He kept them all as his servants.
To make his own decisions, he built the Akal Takht in front of the Golden Temple. Father to the first Jathedar Parbandhak Bhai Gurdas Ji. The Guru said, "This will not be an ordinary throne! No one will sit here and take sides. Full justice will be done. The whole arrangement will be made by sitting on this throne? | When Guru Sahib himself sat on the throne, he put on saffron bana and adorned his head with beautiful dassar! He also ordered that from now on, after Sodar's outpost, the warriors 'warriors' verses would be sung so that cowardice could be removed from the Sikhs and courage could be instilled.
All disputes between the Sikhs were decided by sitting on the Akal Takht. Guru Sahib would make a quick decision after listening to both the parties and their decision would have to be accepted by both the parties in any case.
When the army was greatly increased, the Guru planned to build a fort to guard the city of Amritsar. Lohgarh Fort on the west side of the city

When Nawab Murtaza Khan of Lahore saw that Guru Ji had also built a fort and the army had greatly increased, he warned Jahangir that Guru Hargobind was increasing his military strength to avenge the martyrdom of his father. Jahangir also feared that the Sikhs might take over the Punjab. So he sent Wazir Khan and Cha Beg to Amritsar to fetch the Guru. | Wazir Khan told Guru Ji that Jahangir only wanted to meet him. The Guru agreed to go with them. When Jahangir appeared, Jahangir said, "I am ill, you are a divine fakir, so stay in Gwalior for a month and pray for my recovery." | The Guru understood that it was all a ploy. He was sent to Gwalior Jail. Many kings were already imprisoned there. Guru Ji even went to the prison and put Mars in Changal He would sing kirtan and recite hymns at both times, then teach the kings to live in Chaddi Kala. Hardas, the jail warden, also became his devotee. Chandu once sent a poisonous costume to kill the Guru. The druggist did not give it to the Guru, but told the Guru about Chandu's move and asked him to be more careful. | When the Guru did not return for a long time, the Guru's family and the Sikh community became very sad. The desire to meet the Guru increased so much that the Sikhs would reach Gwalior and return after bowing to the walls of the fort. | Sai Mian Mir from Lahore was a great devotee of Guru's house. He had seen with his own eyes Guru Arjan being tortured and martyred.

When they found out about the imprisonment of Guru Hargobind, they were not released and reached Delhi. There he met many eminent Sufi fakirs of Delhi. | There they found out that Jahangir had married Noor Jahan. Noor Jahan was a resident of Lahore and a devotee of Sai Mian Mir. Meet Sai Mian Mir Noor Jahan. In those days Jahangir was very ill and was not recovering even with the treatment of great physicians. King Jahangir was also pleased to meet Mian Mir and said to him, 'You are the guardian of Allah, from my health.

Pray for Sai Mian Mir said, "You have tortured and killed a divine light and kept its divine son in captivity. Unless you can get rid of them, give up the idea of recovery. Jahangir also had a thought in his mind. He was very sorry that he had killed an innocent fakir and imprisoned his son. | He immediately issued the royal decree that Guru Hargobind should be released. But when Wazir Khan took the order and reached Gwalior, the rest of the Rajo became very sad. He requested Guru Ji to release him also. The Guru told Wazir Khan that he would not leave the jail until all the other prisoners were released. Jahangir again sent orders that all the kings who could grab his skirt and go out would be released. Hearing this, the Guu made a costume of 52 strings and had all the kings released with him. Kings are called 'captives' because of their redemption.

Jahangir had ordered Nawab Wazir Khan to release the Guru and bring him to Delhi. Jahangir regretted that the innocent fakir had tortured and martyred Guru Arjan. He wanted to put the blame on Chandu and other rulers. So he wanted to meet Guru Hargobind and acquit himself. He called the Guru and seated him with great reverence! King Jahangir said, "I was misinformed that you want to avenge your father, you are making military preparations for this, but my misunderstanding has gone away. The culprit is Chandu, I have imprisoned him and his family. They will be handed over to you. But the Guru knew who the real culprit was, he did not consider Jahangir innocent.

Emperor Jahangir now wanted to establish good relations with the Guru. So he requested Guru Sahib to stay with him for a few days. The Guru stayed at Majnu Ke Tilla. Now Jahangir and Guru Sahib used to go hunting together One day a terrible lion appeared in front of them. Jahangir said that there is a warrior who can face this lion. But none of Jahangir's warriors could dare. Then the Guru jumped up and appeared in front of the lion. When the lion roared and struck them, they slammed their shields into his mouth so that the lion ate the bhuatni and fell on the rocks. Then they cut the lion in two with their swords. Jahangir was shocked to see this. I had never seen such a hero before. He really wanted to be killed by the lion when Guru Ji would fight the lion but the lion could not hurt him.

n addition to hunting, there were sometimes archery competitions. plants were planted in the Yamuna river and they were shot with arrows. Every arrow of the Guru would hit the target. The king was amazed at their amazing shooting.

A Ghahi lived in Delhi. He was very devoted to the Guru's house and wanted to see the Guru. But in Delhi he could not meet Guru Ji One day he found out that Guru Ji had gone hunting. He too lovingly cut the grass and walked towards the forest. He went into the forest and saw two different tents

He did not know in which tent the Guru was resting. By mistake he went to Jahangir's camp. The guards first stopped him but later released him as a plaintiff Going in front of the king's bhambu, he laid down the bundle of grass and placed one taka in front of Jahangir and bowed down. Then he said, "True king, help me in this world and in the next world, in the end I have only your support." Can't help you. "Hearing this, Ghahi realized that he had come to the wrong place. He picked up his taka and a bundle of grass and went to another camp When he saw the Guru, he fell at his feet and begged, "My true king, I have gone to the wrong place, forgive me." Ordered to recite from the heart. Ghahi was very happy and went away blessing the Guru. Jahangir was very impressed by this sight and in his eyes the respect for Guru Ji increased even more!

When Guru Ji started marching towards Punjab, the emperor handed over Chandu and his family to Guru Ji. The Guru asked Chandu's family to leave. They also wanted to pardon Chandu, but the Sikhs insisted that they would take Chandu with them. Seeing the wrath of the Sikhs, they handed over Chandu to Bhai Bidhi Chand and Bhai Jetha. When Guru Ji reached Amritsar, great joy was celebrated On the night of Diwali, lamps were lit in the Golden Temple and fireworks were set off. Sikh sangats came from far and wide to visit. | After staying in Amritsar for some time, he went to Lahore to meet Sai Mian Mir. There all the Pir Fakirs came to meet him. While Guru Ji was preaching in Lahore city, Bhai Bidhi Chand and Bhai Jetha Chandu were also taken to Lahore. | When the people of Lahore saw Chandu, he got angry and whoever saw him would hit him in the head. In this way the moon was humiliated. Shells were hurriedly ordered from him. Passing through the streets like this, when he reached the shop of Kurbhunja from which Chandu had poured hot sand on Guru Ji, he became very angry. He put the burning Chet on Chandu's head. Chandu got up and started screaming. The scoundrel said, "When the same sand was poured on Satguru's head, he did not sneeze and you are killing." Now there is no shame. He fell to the ground. His body was then dumped on the riverbank for dog food. | After staying in Lahore for some time, the Guru returned to Amritsar. Having befriended Patshah Jahangir, the Guru no longer had any fear.

But they wanted to strengthen their military power, because kings are never friends with anyone. Those who can kill their brothers and sons, what do they think?

So he built a solid wall around Amritsar. To Lohgarh Fort Confirmed anew. After staying in Amritsar for some time, the Guru made up his mind to go and preach in the villages of Majha. One day they were on their way to the village of Chabbe when a mother named Sulakhni Ji surrounded the Guru's horse.

Mata Sulakhni was a resident of Chabbe village and had no children at home. She had passed many Sadh Fakirs, but her wish was not fulfilled.

When people told her that Satguru Hargobind Sahib, the owner of Miri Peeri, was coming to Chabbe village, she would stand in the way with pen and ink.

Calling the Guru's horse, she began to say, No one is left empty-handed, give me the gift of a son to the poor. " The Guru said, "The gift of a son is not written in your writings." Mai Sulakhni began to say with great confidence, "You should have written the article there too, you have to write here too." When the Guru started writing "੧" on his hand, the horse shook his foot and "ੲ " was written instead. History testifies that true sons were born in that mother's house and they continued to serve the Guru's house a lot.

After preaching Sikhism in Majha for some time, Guru Ji went to Doaba. Kartarpur Nagar, Guru Arjan had already settled. The Guru went to Kartarpur and pitched his tent. When the sangats of Doaba came to know about it, they rushed to Darshan. The Gur remained at Kartarpur when some Pathans, led by Ismail Khan, approached the Guru for employment. They were all Chhabi Pathans and Guru Ji met them alone and kept them in his army. One of these Pathans was Gilji Gabhru. That handsome young man came with his widowed mother to see the Guru. The Guru, seeing her huddled body, kept her with him. They took some jagir in the name of his mother and built a house for her residence. The young boy's name was Pande Khan. The Guru took upon himself the responsibility of raising Painde Khan. The milk of two manjhas was reserved exclusively for him and no account was kept of the number of almonds and other fruits he ate.

Ismail Khan, a prominent warrior, was entrusted with the task of teaching him martial arts. When Guru Ji himself got the time, he kept explaining to Pandey Khan many wonderful relics of martial arts. A few years later, Pandey Khan became a visionary wrestler and a valiant warrior. His games were the only ones to watch. People were amazed.

He had so much power in his hands that he could only erase the letter engraved on the silver rupee by rubbing it with his finger. Holding it in one hand, he would double the rupee,

He used to carry the buffalo or the oxen on his shoulders with his legs tied. His most amazing game was that no matter how hard the rider came running, he would stop the horse and turn both the horse and the rider upside down. People used to come with great enthusiasm to see his bravery and his amazing games. His bravery came to light when in the first battle of the Sikhs, Didar Ali, a companion of Mukhlis Khan, was killed in a single rush as he came out of the fort of Lohgarh and shouted at the Mughal troops. In front of him the Mughal armies fled like sheep.

The Guru praised him for his bravery in this battle. But this compliment had the opposite effect on him. He became so arrogant that he began to realize that the Guru had won because of him.

In the fourth battle which took place at Kartapur, he fought against Guru Sahib. He forgot the favors of Guru Ji and got ready to fight against Guru Ji behind a small eagle. No matter how brave he considered himself, he alone was afraid to clash with the Guru. | So he met the governor of Lahore who sent Kale Khan with a large army to attack the Guru. Kale Khan was killed in this fierce battle. Pandey Khan, boasting of his bravery, came to fight the Guru. The Guru said to him, "Painde khan, pahil teri hai baar kar, pande khan struck with all force, but Guru ji stopped Sehaj Subha." The Guru asked him to strike again. This is how Pandey Khan did three times which was stopped by Guru Ji.

Then the Guru made such a blow that he fell off the horse. The Guru dismounted from his horse and carried him to another world. Thus ended the arrogant Khan.

Bibi Kaulan was the daughter of a Qazi named Rustam Khan of Lahore. He was very clever in dexterity and dexterity. When he completed his primary education, the Qazi sent him to Sai Mian Mir for higher studies. | Sai Mian Mir was very fond of Guru Ghar. He used to visit Amritsar regularly and discuss spirituality with Guru Arjan and later with Guru Hargobind. When Guru Ji also went to Lahore, he would definitely go to the dera of Sai Mian Mir. He also enjoyed spiritual bliss by reciting Guru Nanak's Bani. In this way he memorized many of Guru Sahib's words orally. When Bibi Kaulan came to read to him, Sai Mian Mir would also inform him about Guru Nanak's Bani. Bibi Kaulan also enjoyed reading Guru's Bani. Due to his love for Bani, he memorized many Bani orally. Sometimes she would recite this hymn at home and also recite it to her mother.
One day the words of Guru Nanak's Bani fell in the ears of Qazi The Qazi was a devout Muslim. He considered the Sikh Gurus as infidels. So he stopped his daughter from reading the Bani. Bibi Kaulan would now recite the Bani in secret or in the absence of the Qazi. She used to request Sai Mian Mir many times that she wanted to see Guru Ji.

Once when Guru Ji went to see Sai Mian Mir, Bibi Kaulan was fortunate enough to see Guru Ji. Seeing the Guru, she became blessed and her desire to become a Sikh became strong in her mind. | One day in her merriment she forgot that Qazi Rustam Khan was at home. She was so imbued with the Guru's color that she began to sing the hymns aloud in a very melodious voice. When the sound of his recitation reached the ears of the Qazi, the Qazi on hearing this became a ball of fire. He started beating his daughter for a stick Finally, after begging, Bibi Kaulan's mother released her. But what effect does such beatings have on God's loved ones? She used to read Gurbani all the time now. When the qazi saw that even beating did not work, he consulted with the other qazis and decided to execute his daughter Kaulan. When Bibi Kaulan's mother found out about this, she was a girl

She left the camp of Sai Mian Mir and told him the whole story. Sai Mian Mir knew that Nawab Wazir Khan and Emperor Jahangir were friends of Guru Hargobind, so he came up with the idea of sending Bibi Kaulan to Amritsar. Sai Mian Mir immediately called Shah Abdul Yar and sent Bibi Kaulan to Amritsar through him. Guru Hargobind arranged a separate house for him. There Bibi Kaulan would recite Bani all the time and keep on chanting the Lord's Name. One day Bibi Kaulan was fortunate enough to visit the Guru's palace. There she was very happy to see the Guru's beloved children. She played with them all day.

But when she returned home, she was sad. She began to think that if she had married the Guru she would have had a son too. One day when Guru Ji went to visit Bibi Kaulan, instead of Chaddi Kala, he was surprised to see her sad. When he asked the reason, Bibi Kaulan expressed her desire. The Guru said, "These sons and daughters are born and die. We will give you a son who will live forever. Then they will take bath in Amrit Sarovar. Mata Kaulan was happy to hear this.

Earlier, only the royal family and the emperor hunted and Hindus were not allowed to hunt. Many forests were reserved for the royal families to hunt. One day the Sikhs too, while hunting, reached the forest where the royal family was hunting. The Sikhs saw an instrument of the royal hunters approaching a prey. They left their eagle behind him. The eagle of the Sikhs threw down the eagle of the royal hunters and the prey caught itself and came down. When a batch of royal hunters approached the Sikhs, they caught the eagle. When the royal hunters came to get their falcon back from the Sikhs, they refused. When he threatened to fight, he said, "We have no fear of fighting. We are not afraid of anyone.
The royal hunter lodged a complaint with the Governor of Lahore, Kulij Khan. He said, "Today he has touched the instrument, tomorrow he will get the crown." Kulij Khan sent 7,000 troops under the command of Mukhlis Khan to reform the Sikhs.

When the Guru heard of the arrival of the imperial forces, he ordered the Sikhs to take charge of the front. On the third day, it was decided that Bibi Viro's wedding would take place in Amritsar. The Guru immediately delivered the Guru Granth Sahib and his family to Jhabal and also sent a message to Bibi Viro's father-in-law that Janj should come to Jhabal. Jhabal also sent food and drink items. | First, near Pipli Sahib, the Imperial Army clashed with the People's Army. It was the first war in which the people were fighting for freedom on the one hand and the army of tyrants on the other. In the battle of Pipli, Bibi Bhani was martyred while fighting valiantly.

The Mughal army again advanced towards the fort and besieged it. The Guru had also left his family and returned to the fort. He ordered a stone cannon to be fired. This stone cannon was made by a leading artisan of Khemkaran by cutting down a dry tree. When the stones in this cannon started falling on the Mughals, then the Mughals began to fall on their heads. The army's legs were dislocated and they started running backwards. Mukhlis Khan again challenged the royal army and said, "Running in front of a group of fakirs.You are not ashamed. In the royal army, they woke up again and fought until it was dark. The next day, the war horn sounded Pandey Khan took command of the Sikh army and marched out of the fort, trampling the Mughals underfoot. Everything that came in front of him was gone at once.

Pandey Khan then challenged Didar Ali, a companion of Mukhlis Khan. Didar Ali was also counted among the select warriors of the Mughal army. When he came across Pandey Khan, he was killed for the first time. Mukhlis Khan again challenged the Guru for a double battle. The Guru accepted his challenge and all the other warriors retreated. The Guru shot the first arrow and the face passed through the horse of Mukhlis Khan. Mukhlis Khan fell down! The Guru also dismounted and confronted Mukhlis Khan. Mukhlis Khan angrily did it three times which was stopped by Guru Ji on his shield. Then he himself did such a thing that the sword cut Mukhlis Khan's pulse and also cut his body in two. After the fall of Mukhlis Khan, the Mughal forces fled.

After winning the first battle with great pomp, Guru Ji came to Jhabal and performed the marriage of Bibi Viro without any fear according to the Gur Maryada. Idle from marriage, he reached Goindwal on his own. Goindwal Aap Ji received a lot of respect. When requested by Guru Amar Das's family to stay longer, he left his women and children there and moved to Kartarpur. Mata Kaulan was living in Kartarpur in those days. The Guru was informed of his illness. When the Guru visited him, he was preparing to go to the next world. After seeing the Guru, she regained consciousness and placed her head at the feet of the Guru, saying, Built in Kartarpur which still exists.

The sangat continued to perform kirtan for many days in memory of Mata Kaulan. . When Jahangir handed over Chandu to Guru Hargobind, his property was also confiscated. The Guru re-established his village Ruhela and renamed it Sri Hargobindpur. After the funeral of Mata Kaulan, when Guru Ji came to Sri Hargobindpur from Kartarpur, he came across Bhagwan Das Gherar. Bhagwan Das used to collect the revenue of Sri Hargobindpur and submit it to the state of Jalandhar. One day he brought some goons with him to drive Guru Ji out of Sri Hargobindpur. He started threatening the Guru with his goons. When the Sikhs found out, they cut it in two and threw it into the river Beas. When his son Ratan Chand found out, he approached Abdullah Khan, the ruler of Jalandhar. He was already against the Guru, so he arrived with four thousand troops to attack Sri Hargobind. When the Guru came to know of this, he too ordered the Sikhs to take charge of the front. As the army approached, the Sikhs rained down such arrows that the imperial army began to flee for their lives. Abdullah Khan held his army hostage till night but the mercenaries kept saving their lives. The next day, Abdullah Khan led an army with his two sons. He sent and said, "Arrest the Sikh fronts without letting the arrows fly." But before he could capture the fronts, his two sons, Nabi Bakhsh and Karim Bakhsh, were killed when Abdullah learned that his two sons When they were killed, he tore through the Sikh army and ran in front of the Guru

Abdullah began to strike the Guru blindly, but the Guru kept his blows on his shield. When Abdullah got tired of doing the blows, the Guru struck with the dagger so hard that Abdullah Khan fell asleep on the ground in two pieces. Chandu's son Karam Chand then came before the Guru to avenge his father's death. When the Guru attacked him with the sword, the Guru's sword broke. Guru Ji didn't think it was right to kill him with Peeri's sword and he stopped washing it then they slapped him so hard that he fell down and lost his breath. Thus the Guru also won this battle.

When King Shah Jahan found out about the defeat, he ordered the city to be demolished. But when he was told by Wazir Khan, "The Guru was building a mosque for the Muslims living in the city which was stopped by Bhagwan Das. This thing. On hearing this, Shah Jahan ordered the confiscation of the property of the ruler of Jalandhar.

The Guru himself did not write the Bani due to his involvement in wars and battles but he respected the Bani very much. When kirtan was performed, they listened with great love. The minds became so concentrated that the existence of the outside world was forgotten. One day the court was closed and the Guru was preaching to the Sikhs after the kirtan. Pointing out the importance of reciting Buddha Bani, he said, The pure reciter also receives the Guru's happiness! ".

While teaching, he stopped and said, "Is there any such Sikh among you? Is the one who can recite the pure recitation of Japji Sahib.

There was silence in the court for a long time and no Sikh dared to claim to be a pure reader. Although hundreds of Sikhs memorized the text of Jap Ji Sahib, everyone was reluctant to recite it to the Guru.

After some time, Bhai Gupala got up and stood up. He said, "I do not claim to have the pure text, but I will try. The rest should be the grace of Aap Ji, the pure text is done automatically. The Guru allowed him to recite. The Guru was sitting on the side of the bed at that time.

Bhai Gupala began to recite the pure text with such concentration that the sangat became merry. Everyone was swaying along with the drink. The Guru, on the other hand, was slipping from the pillow to the foot while listening to the text.

The Guru was thinking in his mind that if he recited it with such concentration and accuracy then I would give him the gur-gaddi, but when Bhai Gupala reached the last step his concentration of mind was also disturbed. He began to think that the Guru would be pleased with my pure reading and say to me, 'Bhai Gupala! You have done the lesson with great concentration, we are very happy with you, ask what you ask for? Then what should I ask for? I should ask for the horse which Subhaga has offered to Guru Ji. In these verses Bhai Gupala Ji recited the Salok of Japji Sahib. The Guru who used to slide towards the feet then turned towards the pillow.

The Guru began to say, "When Bhai Gupala started reciting, he lost his mind which was connected with lord.

 At that time we made up our mind that we would give him the gur-gaddi but when we reached the last steps, his desire went to the Chinese horse. We give that Chinese horse to Bhai Paale as a reward.

Then Guru Ji started addressing Bhai Gupale and said, But the attraction of worldly things brought you down instead of the union of the Lord. Now you just imagined a horse, the horse is present. '

Bhai Gupale accepted these words of Guru Sahib and said, "Guru Ji is right, how can we worldly beings rise at once to compete with the saints and great men. , Are free from anger, greed, attachments and ego. But the Guru, leaning on him, said, "Whoever recites with sincerity in the Guru's house is a saint.

The one who recites the verses becomes a Mahatma. You were about to snatch the mattress from us, it was all the result of your concentration.

The battle of Sri Hargobindpur greatly encouraged the Sikhs of Doaba After the death of Abdullah Khan, the atrocities in Doaba came to an end. The Guru stayed in the city for a few days. He built a wall and demolished the house of Bhagwan Das and built a mosque. In those days Baba Buddha Ji's message reached Aap Ji that his last time is near so let him visit! Baba Buddha was 125 years old at that time.

As soon as the message was received, Guru Hargobind reached Ramdas village Baba Buddha. Baba Buddha was very happy to see Guru Ji. The Guru said, "Dhan Baba ji! You have enjoyed the company of five Gurus and have been fortunate enough to see and serve Guru Nanak. You have shown the world that even an ordinary human being becomes a Bahmagiani by implanting the Guru Shabad in his Hirda. The next day Baba Buddha Ji merged with the Lord like a snake's key. After completing the worldly rites, he decorated the turban of Baba Bhana, the nephew of Baba Buddha, and gave him the throne of Baba Buddha.

From Ramdas, the Guru crossed the Kartarpur Ravi river, where he met the grandchildren of Guru Nanak and went to his village Bathe to meet Baba Sri Chand. The Guru was accompanied by Baba Gurditta and Baba Suraj Mal at that time. Baba Sri Chand Ji was very happy to meet Guru Hargobind Sahib. Guru Ji along with his two sons went to

Baba Ji. Guru Ji kept telling Baba Ji about wars and battles. But Baba Sri Chand's attention was on Sahibzada Gurditta Ji. His face looked exactly like Guru Nanak's. Then Baba Sri Chand Ji started saying, "How many Sahibzada's do you have?" When Guru Ji told him that there are five, Baba Ji started saying, Guru Ji said, "The five belong to Baba Ji, take whichever one of them."

Then Baba Sri Chand Ji grabbed Gurditta's hand and said, "This is your Tikka too, so is our Tikka too, so now it has become the Tikka of Deen Duni." And began to say, "Guru Nanak's gift of my old age has already gone to your house, this fakir was with me,

It also gave you.

The Guru was very pleased and said, "Great men, this is all your blessing." From that day onwards, people started calling Mr. Gurditta as Baba's groom, "Baba Gurditta, Tikka of Deen Duni". In this way Baba Sri Chand passed on his 110 years of earnings to Baba Gurditta. In this way a solid tool for the propagation of Sikhism was acquired. Guru Ram Dass ji had humbly fallen in love with Baba ji, and Gur Hargobind surrendered his son to him, embracing the sad death. Later, the Udasi sect did much to promote Sikhism.

When the Sikh Panth was going through great difficulties and its very existence was in danger, the Udasis went from house to house preaching Sikhism. That is why it is a historical event that Baba Sri Chand made Baba Gurditta Ji his successor.

At that time Baba Sri Chand had four major dhunis (preaching centers) in the country. Baba Sri Chand Ji handed over these four incense sticks to Baba Gurditta. These were the main characters of the four sounds; Baba Almasat Ji, Baba Balu Hasona, Baba Goinda and Baba Phool Ji.

Hundreds of Muslims were also drawn to Guru Hargobind. Khwaja Roshan was a devout Muslim fakir. Hundreds of people flocked to his camp every day to collect firewood. But Khwaja Roshna's mind was not stable. He himself was in search of a Murshad whom he could find peace of mind. He heard the Guru's praise from a friend and came to the Guru. He was so happy to hear the Guru's words that he stayed with the Guru forever. His heart did not want to be away from the Guru. He was always in the ministry. He also looked after the Guru's horses. One day, when the Gur rode away on horseback, he was terrified that the Gur would not go away from him; He too ran after the Guru's horse. For a mile he chased after the Guru's horse. When Guru Ji realized that Khwaja Roshan was running after him, he stopped his horse. He dismounted and took the Khwaja Ration in his arms and said, "You have now got everything you wanted to get!" Appointed masand for preaching.
Khwaja Roshan used to go from village to village preaching Sikhism. One day while Khwaja was preaching Sikhism, he met Sanyad Jani Shah. Syed Jani Shah was also wandering again for peace of mind.

He had met many Sufi saints and fakirs but his heart was not satisfied. Khwaja Roshan understood his state of mind and began to say, "It seems that Jani has not got Jani yet. If you want to meet your Jani then meet Guru Hargobind and they will reunite you with your Jani." At first Jani Shah could not believe it but when Khwaja Roshan told his own and some people's stories, Jani Shah got full confidence. He walked to the Guru's door. Sitting outside the door, he started shouting, "Jani ko jani mila do ji." She kept this all day. But Guru Ji did not pay any attention to him and did not get any inquiry from anyone as to who was shouting loudly Of Allah

There will be visions that come back tired of points, then nothing will happen. Guru Ji ignored him and had bricks laid in front of him so that the curtain
Be done But he did not move from his place and the only thing he shouted was, "Give life to life. When he did not stop speaking, the Guru sent him a bag of money through a Sikh. He did not look at Bailey nor towards the Sikh. When he did not even take the bag of money, the Guru sent a message through the Sikh, "If it is too early, jump into the river." | Hearing this, Jani ran towards the river. The Guru sent some horsemen after him to bring him back. As the Sikhs approached, they jumped into the river. The Sikhs also jumped after him and grabbed him and brought him out The Sikhs on horseback presented him before the Guru.

The Gurugot up, embraced him to his bosom and blessed him with Naam Daan. With the Guru's hand his mind became calm and he got everything! When the Guru saw that he had now become one with his Allah and that Jani had found Jani, they engaged him in preaching.

Bhai Gurdass ji was living in Goindval in his last days.
Bhai Gurdass ji was a person who had been preaching Sikhism since the time of Guru Amar Dass. He was born in the village of Basarke, near Amritsar, in the year 1612 B.C. He was the nephew of Guru Amar Das. When Gur Amar Dass settled the town of Goindval, Guru Angad ordered him and his family to settle in Goindval. Guru Amar Das came with all his brothers and their families. He also had a nephew, Bhai Gurdas, in his family. Guru Amar Das gave Bhai Gurdas a very high education. Educated in the Guru's Satsang, he became a great scholar of Punjabi, Hindi, Sanskrit and Bijbhasha. After receiving his education, he preached Sikhism with great humility, devotion and dedication. He taught many, waters, Simran, Seva and Parupkaar.
Guru Arjan Dev Ji bestowed upon him the greatest honor of having the first volume of Guru Granth Sahib written by him. He worked very hard to write this Bir. Only by writing this Bir did you gain divine wisdom.
He was also a poet of high caliber.

He composed his poems in Punjabi and wrote poems and poems in Bijbhasha. Aap Ji's Bani has the status of the key of Guru Granth Sahib. The key is to say that Aap's creation Gurbani works to unravel and clarify the two hidden meanings and secrets. He has explained Gurmat Darshan, Gur Bhagti, Gurmukh's position, Manmukh's identity, Gurmat ethics and morality in his verses.

When Akbar started practicing his new religion, Din-e-Ilahi, he invited scholars of different religions and went to Agra to present the doctrine of Sikhism. He had also nailed the heads of all religions along with his erudition. He had also gone to Banaras to eradicate the influence of Pandits and to preach Sikhism . When Guru Hargobind established the Akal Takht, he was appointed the first Jathedar of the Akal Takht. They were, 'Bhai Sam Nahi Sikh and Mum Bhai! When the Gur sat on the Akal Takht, he would hold it by the arm and sit next to it.

When Bhai Gurdass realized that his last days were approaching, he sent a message to Gur Hargobind. Upon receiving his message, the Guru left all work and reached Goindval. When he finally got Guru Ji with him, Bhai Ji's face blossomed like a red rose. The Guru asked the Sikhs for Bani Pan and he sat down next to Bhai Ji. Bhai Gurdas Ji once again looked at the Guru. The Guru reassured them that they had now arrived. Then Bhai Ji would say, 'My last time is near. Ordering the Sikh Sangat that when my dreams come true, they should chant Waheguru, make no cremation for me, offer my flowers and ashes to the river Beas. After some time, Bhai Gurdas Ji passed away. The coffin of Bhai Gurdas was turned on one side by Guru Hargobind Sahib and Baba Bhana Ji and on the other side by Bhai Jetha Ji and Bhai Bidhi Chand.

Once the Sangat of Kabul came to Guru Darshan, they were accompanied by Bhai Karori Mal who brought a good breed of horse Gulbag and Dilbag to present to Guru Ji! While all this sangat was roaming around Lahore, the eyes of Anait-ulla, the ruler of Lahore, fell on those horses. Anaitullah wanted to get the price of the horse, but Crore Mal refused saying that he had brought the horse not for sale but to present to his beloved Guru Hargobind Sahib. The ruler got angry at this and snatched the two horses. When the sangat of Kabul reached the Guru, all the sangats bowed down with but instead of putting forward the offerings, they said in a sad tone, But they were lost on the way by Anait-ul-Ula, ruler of Lahore; I have nothing left to offer you now. The Guru consoled him and said with a laugh, "Your horses have reached us, we will bring them ourselves now." Don't worry, we are very happy with you, we will release you only after receiving your precious gift. Bhai Karori Mal was satisfied and he was happy.

Guru Ji called Bidhi Chand to his side. He slapped him and prayed in the name of five Gurus and sent him to Lahore. Bidhi Chand reached Lahore and stayed at Bhai Jeevan's house The next day he disguised himself as a weeder and after digging and shaking off a bundle of fine grass, Saide Khan, a horse dropper, who was sitting near the outer wall of the fort, when he came out, he was very happy to see good grass, but the grass was also cheap. And even happier when we met. He took Bidhi Chand to the royal stables to carry the horses and put them on the horses! Bhai Bidhi Chand kept on giving grass to the horses and also gave them love by caressing them. Bhai Bidhi Chand used to bring hay every day and feed the horses. By taking care of this daily service, the horses also started recognizing Bhai Bidhi Chand and when he brought hay, he would whine. Seeing the love of Bhai Bidhi Chand, Saide Khan hired him as a servant for the service of horses. He himself used to be very naive but his message was spread day by day with horses. They throw out a big rock every night

The river Ravi was flowing touching the walls of the fort. The watchmen could not see anything when they heard the sound of stones being thrown. Eventually they realized that an animal was coming against the wall of the fort, so they became obsessed with it. Bidhi Chand used to leave his salary to the guards. They were very happy with them. When Bidhi Chand received his next salary, the guards had to be fed so much that they fainted. Bidhi Chand locked them in a room. Then the horse with the keys opened Gulbagh and removed it from behind and killed him by jumping so hard that he jumped over the fort including Bidhi Chand and jumped into the river. Bhai Bidhi Chand presented the horse to the Guru. The Guru highly praised Bhai Bidhi Chand in the full congregation. The second horse was brought by Bidhi Chand Najumi. When he reached Guru Ji with the other horse, Guru Ji put him on his chest and said:

ਬਿਧੀ ਚੰਦ ਛੀਨਾ। ਗੁਰੂ ਕਾ ਸੀਨਾਂ.

Third Sikh War was fought.

When the two horses reached Guru Ji, Guru Ji warned that there would be another war. When Bidhi Chand came with the second horse, he shouted, "These two horses belonged to Guru Hargobind. I took the first horse and I am taking the second horse." Let's catch it if it's released. "

A young man with two horses and so many guards from the royal stables of a powerful government. ' What is the honor of such a government?

So the Guru began preparations for war. The Guru was living in the Malwa at that time. He asked Bheri Rai Jodha of the area, "You know this area, tell me a place where a small army can defeat many enemies." Rai Jodh told them many locations but Guru Ji chose Nathana's hill as a good place to fight. The beauty of this place was that on one side there was a slope and on the other three sides there were mountain rails. It is also important to control the water during war. From Lahore, news reached Bhai Bohru that Anair-ul-Ula had sent Lalla Beg and Kamra Beg to the Malwa with an army of ten thousand. When the army was approaching the Malwa, Kabli Beg joined them on the way. In this way the number of the royal army increased even more. Rai Jodh was leading the Guru's army. The whole army numbered about three thousand. But when the drum sounded, the Guru's beloved joined the Guru's army with whatever weapon he could get his hands on. Lalla Beg also approached while searching

Vasdo sent Hasan Khan to get the Guru's information. The Sikhs seized him on arrival. But the Guru released him. When he returned, he told the roaring bag that the Guru's forces were ready to fight the green attack.

When Lalla Beg found out that the water was in Guru's possession, he went to the wormhole to find water. The Sikhs rained bullets on the right occasions. The imperial army was alarmed by the sudden onslaught. The people who ran after them used to get salt water from wells for drinking, which made a large part of the royal army sick. Fighting had been going on all night and in the morning Lalla Beg saw it

There were corpses all around. Lala Beg was furious and took over the command of the army. The Guru was guiding the troops sitting on the high hill. Lalla Beg, Kamar Beg and Kabli Beg all advanced. It started raining arrows from both sides. Seeing all this, Kabli Beg stepped forward and challenged Guru Ji! The Guru told him to strike, "When Kabli Beg struck, the Guru was injured. Then, in a fit of rage, he fired an arrow that split Kabli Beg in two. Seeing Kabli Khan falling, Kamar Beg stepped forward Guru Ji's wounds were bandaged by Rai Jodh and he proceeded to fight Then Rai Jodh wielded such a sword that Kamar Beg was also killed. Lalla Beg again stepped forward. Herb came forward to stop him but was killed. Guru Ji then proceeded on his own, Lalla Beg released the arrow, but Guru Ji again stopped the arrow on Guru's hair and shot such an arrow that his horse fell down. Laila Beg then started walking again. The Guru dismounted and confronted him. The duel began. But Guru ji did such a thing that Lalla Beg was torn in two. After the death of Lalla Beg, there was panic in Turkey. The Guru treated the wounded and conducted the cremation of the martyrs under his supervision.

Lola Beg's spy Hassan Khan survived. Hasan Khan remained among the Sikhs as a spy for Jahan and by observing the conduct of the Sikhs he too became a disciple of the Guru. To assuage the anger of Emperor Shah Jahan, he gathered the remaining army and took it to Lahore. The emperor had come to Lahore at that time. Wazir Khan, who had won the Guru's battle, was also very happy. He approached the king and said, "Lalla Beg, who had gone to get back two horses, did not know whether he had returned or not. At the same time Solabat Khan Deori Bardar pleaded, "Sir, Hasan Khan has come from the battlefield, call him and ask him. Hasan Khan was summoned to the court at that time. The king asked, "What happened to Laila Beg?"
Hasan Khan began to say, "King Hazur, if you have given your life, I will tell you all the circumstances."
Hasan Khan said, "Lalla Beg and Kamar Beg quickly reached the place where the Guru was staying. But that area was all forest. Due to lack of first provision, drinking water was not available and after drinking salty hoof water all the young men and horses got sick.

Only wild people could be seen there, nowhere near the village. There was a mound of water which the Guru had earlier occupied We begged Lola Beg not to go any further, but she accepted one of our names and led the army into the thorny bushes. As soon as he left, fighting broke out and the Sikhs were killed. Then he showed the hand that the royal army had changed. The torches were lit and attacked again but such a cold wind blew that the torches were extinguished and the cold cold numbed the royal army. Hands and feet became numb and guns and swords fell from the hands of the soldiers. The whole army fell unconscious. The Sikhs could have killed the whole army overnight if they wanted to, but their Guru has commanded that whoever strikes should be killed, not the other. Overnight part of the search died and only part remained The next day Lola Beg and Kamar Beg saw the dead Chhej, but now what was presented? Yet he did not give up. We celebrated very much that Guru Ji himself never attacks. Heal the armies

Let them fight again but they did not listen to anyone. They all got drunk and attacked the Sikhs. It is not known where the Sikhs came from in large numbers. Lalla Beg and Kabli Beg were killed by the Guru and the rest of the rulers and army were killed by the Sikhs. When the army saw that all its officers had been killed, they all fled. The Sikhs did not pursue them, but the savages divided and beat them, snatching their horses and clothing.

I have saved two thousand and brought them, the rest of the wounded and half-dead have been taken away by the Guru's Sikhs for treatment. After agreeing, they too will come. Eighteen thousand troops were killed by Lalla Beg's stupidity! Although now we say that we were killed by our own foolishness, but I know that even if the Guru is attacked ten times more than that, he cannot come out victorious. The Guru is the light of God, he can conquer the whole world if he wants to, but he despises government and wealth.

On hearing this, the king was very pleased and at the request of Wazir Khan made Hasan Khan governor of Kabul. Hasan Khan did much service to the Guru by becoming Subedar. He used to send camels of fruits, dhusa, pashmina and other clothes to Guru ji.

After winning the battle, Guru Ji came to his camp, Guru Ji and Rai Jodh sewed their wounds and bandaged them. Within a few days the Guru recovered.

He prepared a fireplace for the Sikhs who were martyred in the war and cremated them together. He buried some of the ashes in Sutlej and buried the rest at the place where Shaheed Ganj now stands. He then gathered the people of the neighboring villages and dug a huge hole in which the bodies of the slain Muslims were thrown and dust was thrown away. Then he made a big platform on it and paved the floor Guru Sahib continued to hold Diwan and kirtan for fifteen days on this Damdamai. Nowadays there is a wave town.The wounded Muslims, when they agreed, were sent to the king of Lahore at their expense. He told the king about the Guru's behavior. Hearing the Guru's praise, the king became convinced that the Guru was a great feather. Shah Jahan was also afraid that it would not be right to fight him because he did not know if he would curse and destroy his kingdom. So the imperial forces did not attack again.

One day Guru Ji, Rai Jodh and other Sikhs went hunting. On the way they saw a huge snake lying on the ground in agony. When that snake saw Guru Ji he got rid of it. When he died then Rai Jodh saw that many worms came out of that snake. Seeing this, Rai Jodh said, "Maharaj! Is it weird that so many worms have come out of a living snake? Hearing this

The Guru said, "He had become a welfare mahant in the previous life. He used to worship from the house of his servants, but he could not save anyone. Instead of devotion to the Lord, he lived a life of asceticism. Just as he used to eat the servants, those people have become worms and eaten his flesh. Now seeing us, he got rid of it. After rescuing the snake, the Guru returned to the camp.

Bhai Rai Jodh, Salem Shah etc. were not allowing Guru Ji to leave Kangar. At last the Guru departed from them and proceeded to Kiratpur through the villages. Along the way, he stopped in several villages to preach. When he reached Gujarwal village, that village

Sardar Fatuhi Grewal did a lot of service to him. One day when he came to Darshan, he brought a chakra in his hand and brought it. The Guru asked him for a sneeze to see his Siddha. Listening to the Guru's words, Fatuhi said, "You have many kinds of gifts from all over the world. I have this shit that I love dearly. Guru Ji spoke! You used to say that my body, mind and wealth belong to the Guru, but I am not ready to give up a single wing. The Guru did not give him that shit and went home ashamed. When he got home and started eating, the snail swallowed the silk cord he was tied to. Fatuhi was still singing when he saw the tormented squirrel. Fatuhi tried hard but the squirrel did not recover. At last he took the stick and went to the Guru and said, "If you fix it, it is yours. When the Guru touched the snail, he untied the rope and healed! Seeing such apparent power, Farruhi Grewal fell at the feet of Guru Ji.

Following the same Gurewal, Guru Ji reached Kiratpur on 22 Baisakh 1669 B.C., preaching Sikhism in villages like Balale, Khamanon, Sanghal, Chamkaur, Ropar etc. Five Kohs from Suraj Mal came forward and met Guru Ji. On reaching Guru ka Mahal, great excitement was celebrated and lamps were lit at night. When the sangat found out that Guru Ji had come to Kiratpur permanently, sangats from all over the country started coming to Darshan. Masand himself started appearing with a car bet. Tikka Baba Gurditta Ji who used to live in Kartarpur also came to Kiratpur. Baba Budhan Shah, a fakir, had been living in Kiratpur since the time of Guru Nanak. They kept goats and took them to graze in the hills during the day. He only drank goat's milk and did not ask for anything from anyone.

Once when Guru Nanak Ji came here, Sai Budhan Shah had placed a strainer of milk in front of him. Guru Nanak Dev Ji had promised at that time that this body Aman was with you, we will definitely come to drink your milk in the sixth jam. Sai Budhan Shah Guru. Nanak became a devotee of Dev and he always prayed that when Guru Ji would come and drink milk from him and save him from birth and death.

One day when Guru Hargobind and Baba Gurditta returned from hunting, they passed by Baba Budhan. The Guru said, "Baba ji! Give us our trusted milk. Baba Budhan Shah looked at him loudly and said, "Jyot looks like Guru Nanak, but the form is not that, if you show that form then I will bring milk. The Guru immediately sent Baba Gurditta to take a bath. When Baba Gurditta came after bathing, his form was exactly like that of Guru Nanak. Sai Budhan Shah was amazed to see the real form of Guru Nanak Dev Ji. Baba Budhan Ji and Guru Hargobind Sahib stood up and said, "Come, Baba Ji Biraj!" One channa was drunk by Guru Hargobind Sahib and another by Baba Gurditta Ji.All doubts of Baba Budhan Shah were dispelled. Whatever question he asks Baba ji He kept getting the right answer. At last Baba Budhan Shah's wish was fulfilled and he gave up his breath. Being a Muslim fakir, Guru Ji dug up his grave and buried him. His grave is still near Baba Gurditta's dera.

In Kiratpur, Darbar was held daily and kirtan was performed at both times. The number of sangats was increasing day by day. The Sikhs had immense devotion to the Guru. At one of their gestures, they were ready to die. One day he called Bhai Jhande. Bhai Jhanda was in charge of the langar. He said to Bhai Jhande, "Tell the Sikhs that whoever brings wood to the langar will be happy." The next day he was carrying firewood. When the Guru saw this, he said, "Bhai Jhande! I told you to go and tell the Sikhs, but you have started collecting firewood yourself? Bhai Jhande replied, "Your order was to tell the Sikhs, so first I am trying to become a Sikh myself."

Once the Guru wandered around and went to Naina Devi. There were many Sikhs with them. They set up camp a short distance from the temple. There all the hill chiefs and other people used to come to visit Naina Devi. In those days the journey of Naina Devi had started. So there were tents all around. Many offerings were made to the temple of Naina Devi and the priests of the temple collected the offerings. | A Sikh by the name of Bhai Bhairon was very happy to see the idol of Naina Devi. It is unknown at this time what he will do after leaving the post. He drew his sword and broke the necklace of the goddess. Then, wielding his sword, he escaped and reached the Guru's camp. There was wailing among the passengers. The complaint came to the mountain king there! Everyone suspected that the culprit of the goddess was hiding in the Guru's camp. The king came and asked the Guru to hand over our culprit. The Guru said, "

Our Sikhs do not lie nor are they afraid that whoever is guilty will come by himself. The priest knew the culprit. So the king asked him to identify the culprit! The priest recognized Bhai Bhairon. Bhai Bhairon said, "I am ready to be punished if justice is done to me, first I must be told what I have done wrong. The priest said, "You have broken the necklace of the goddess. Bhai Bhairon said, "First take me to Devi Mata ji, only then the real thing will be known. The priest is deliberately adding blame on me to save his life." The king and the priests took her to the temple of the goddess. Some Sikhs also went with him to see the reality. Going into the temple, he saw the necklace of the revered goddess without a necklace. Many pilgrims were weeping at the sight of Goddess Mata and the women were weeping. Bhai Bhairon said We ask the Goddess Mata Ji who lost her necklace if I have broken her necklace. Then he folded his hands towards the Goddess and stood up and said, "O Goddess Mata Ji tell the truth whether I have broken your necklace, speak, tell the truth once or else this Pandit has started killing me innocent. At his plea, all the passengers started laughing. This is a fool. "

He said to the king, "Ask me if I have harmed him or someone else, because the real plaintiff is the one who has been harmed." What about the rest? Everyone will say, this is a fool, let him go, he doesn't even know if the goddess speaks or not. " Can't get her own justice, who can't even save herself, what good will she do to anyone?

All the passengers understood that Bhai Bhairon was not a fool but all those fools who did not understand the real thing. The king released Bhai Bhairon.

This proves what morality the Guru's Sikhs possess. Once a person was ready to become a Muslim due to many restrictions in Hinduism, his partner said that there are many restrictions of Shariah in Muslim religion too, there is no restriction in that religion to become a Sikh.

www.ingramcontent.com/pod-product-compliance
Lightning Source LLC
Chambersburg PA
CBHW040216110726
48005CB00019B/3041